i hope this ____ ____
you when you need it most.
may your un.packing journey
be filled with lots of love,
healing + self-discovery
xx amb♡

un.packing

un.packing

A COLLECTION OF POEMS AND PROSE

Aijah Monet

This is a work of creative nonfiction. Some parts have been fictionalized in varying degrees, for various purposes.

Cover Illustration by Andew Peña
Drawings by Mae Kransnewitz
Cover Design by Gisella DelBuono
Editing by Jennifer Sanfilippo
Contributions by Jessica Tumio
Photography by Ike Abakah

ISBN 978-1-7345850-0-1 (paperback)

First Edition
First Edition: March 2020
This paperback edition first published in 2020

Published by Aijah Monet Downer
aijahmonet.com

to my un.packing friends and family
thank you for everything

Your belief in me transformed my world

Prologue

I am okay. I am mostly happy. I am safe. You will
begin reading from a time in my life that is not
now. un.packing is a collection of thoughts,
feelings, and stories that I have translated from the
messy 3 a.m. scribbles that held all the pain in my
world. A time where I stopped speaking and
could only write. You're going to read this and it
is going to hurt you. Please know that I am sorry.
Deeply and truly. So much of me almost threw it
all away because of that realization. I didn't want
to hurt you or scare you or confuse you.
But really, I didn't want you to try and stop me.
I don't know if you know how much your
opinion means to me. But your approval or
disapproval could stop me or give me the green
light for anything. I needed to do this and
I couldn't risk that.

I want you to join me in the pain of un.packing
without resistance. Because when you turn each
page and eventually close this book, you will
know that I am okay. I am happy and I am safe.
I am here and I am happy to be. I have decided to
challenge the pain our culture stifles and chokes
back. The baggage that bruises and strains.
The heaviness that wears us at the base of our

shoulder blades, that darkens our under eyes and turns our hair salt and pepper. The tautness in our being that brews hypertension. The trauma that festers shame and secrecy. You're going to wish I didn't say certain things. That I kept them out or skated over them. I understand why.

This is my truth. I want to be heard. Especially by you, who may feel like I have said too much. My need to be honest, despite it being warranted, is in your hands.

You loved me enough through this pain. More than I deserved or ever made sense. Please don't worry about that. You were enough. The mind of an artist is a flowery one. I make sad words feel like sunshine. You might wonder why or how I got so sad. I'm here to explain, but I hope you see the light strung through every page. Bound by Grace. I hope you find how much my spirit and faith emerges. Know that I have also felt so much love in this life of mine, that without it, these very words could not meet your eyes. I had to fall. Over and over again. Feel excruciating pain. Embarrass myself and probably you too. Burry myself deep in that hole and eventually crawl out. That was something I had to do, in order to reach this part.

un.packing isn't the pretty part. We talked about that. My pain was real. It radiated out of my being the way people now say my light does.
I hope you are proud that I have lived this life so authentically that I have been able to translate the hardest moments in all of our lives into words of healing for hearts in need of mending.

The pretty part, well, that's the part I'm exploring now. I promise we'll get there. You and I together. Someday, you will read a book written by me that portrays me the way I know you see me. The only way you want me to be seen. You may not understand this book, but I just want to tell you I wrote it for us, anyways. I love you so deeply. There is so much of me that gets in the way of that. But please know that it's true.

You lead me so proudly through life I don't know if there is a greater gift I could receive…than to be the child of an elegant warrior. I am your messy flower child. You watched the way un.packing transformed me. How I danced and laughed and woke up happy. Joy flows through me now. Everything you love about that, I ask that you honor in this too. There would be no this without that.

Thank you for keeping me alive. For keeping me safe. Thank you for hugging me when it felt so unnatural. It kind of still does. For forcing affection and love back into my being. For being my mother before my friend. Thank you for loving me despite the pain. I love you despite yours.

Chapter One

In the beginning it was beautiful

Introduction

I've been waiting to find the right
moment to sit down and finally share
my thoughts. This journal, second to
you, is my lifeline. When you're not
there I have an object to turn to.
As sad as that may seem, I can't
imagine sharing these thoughts with
anyone else but you or the lines of
a notebook. I guess I chose tonight
because it's raining and you're not
around and I know these nights a
month from now will be unbearable.
I know that you will be so far away,
so far from me. I know that I will
miss you more than anything on nights
like this a month from now and I
guess that's my reason for writing
tonight. No one will know how
desperately I will wish these lines
were you. Your fingertips, your skin,
your lips, and your mind. No one will
know how close this journal makes me
feel to you. And no matter how much
I write and for how long, nothing can
change how badly I wish you were
there. This is going to be so hard
and it's going to hurt more than
anything I have ever felt but I know
in my heart you will always be there.
In the wind, in the lyrics, in my
meals, in my laughs, in my tears,

in the way I speak. You are so much
a part of me. So, I will write and I
will miss you like hell. It'll burn
like the knot in my throat as I write
this. I will miss you more than
I have ever missed anyone and that
is because I don't know who you'll be
when we see each other next. And
really, I don't know who I'll be.
I want to hold on to the you I know
for as long as I can because one day
it could all change. I will write on
the stormy nights as well as the most
beautiful of days where I wish you
could see just how beautiful things
were. I'll write when I see the moon
and know you see it too. I'll write
when it seems like it's just too much
and this will be all I have. I will
also write when things just seem too
good without you and I'll pray you
don't feel that too. I'll continue to
write as I continue to love you.
Thank you for this book. I wanted it
for so long, but I had no idea it
would make me feel like this. I miss
you tonight just like I will miss you
on so many others. It's hard to
believe one day I may be used to this
feeling and missing you will just be
how it is. I don't regret for a
second falling in love...how could I,
it wasn't my choice. When I met you
there was no stopping whatever was to
come.

Here and there

I closed my eyes and our souls danced.
They danced for the moment.
Slow and close like we do.
Rejoiced in finding each other once again,
and always once again.

Until it was time to say goodbye.
Their time was short in that realm.
That dimension where the mind rarely gazed.

"I miss you."

"I'm right there.

Don't worry.

I'm right there."

"It's beautiful with you *there*. But my love, I can't
wait to meet you *here*."

"For another time my dear…for another time."

aijah monet

Our Love Can Never Die...

I'll keep us alive in my writing, dear.
I don't think we'll make it
any other way.

I'm a Writer.

Now, then, and Always

We will meet again, my friend.
In another time unlike this.
You will be you and I will be me.
Completely unaware of the Pacifics you swam,
The grassy fields I've strolled through,
The wildflowers we've picked.

Will you see me the same?
The way I always hoped you would?
Will you know now?
Will you know in the moment you see me?
All this time later?
I hope you know.
I hope the feeling is so consuming,
All-consuming,
And there is nothing else you do know, but that.

That it's me.
Me, who you want.
Now, Then, and Always.
I hope you're sure of that.
I hope to see you soon, my friend.

Premenstrual Dysphoric Disorder

I'm okay,
but I'm low right now
Coming off a high
I've never felt more alive
The sky is gray, —it's the middle of May
Let's try one more time
Our eyes are dry
Let's try one more time
I'm okay,
but I'm low right now
Sinking
but I haven't drowned
The sky is blue and I miss you too
Pain and joy all in one gulp
Heaven
Hell
Despair and hope
The sky is pale and I reek of ale
Clinging to ideas of sanity
I'm okay,
but I'm low right now
I'll see you again
but I'm on my way down.

to You, Avec Amour, from France
Part I

All I know and all I've ever known is I want my
life with you in it. So that's what I will think
about while I'm here. That is the story I will tell
because that is my truth. That is my truth as it
always has been. So I will finally write the story
I would love to live. Excuse me if I get carried
away. This is raw, honest, and unfiltered, as life
should be. This isn't me watching my words or
diluting my dreams. Here they are. This is me.
This is what I want. These are thoughts and
details I have never said out loud. Thoughts and
details so intricate, I am not sure of what they will
be until I allow myself to have them. I don't know
if these dreams exist outside of you. I'm sure I
could still have them, I'm just not sure if I would
want them. Or at least not this way. I believe that
would be another story. The parallel to my ideal
life. Maybe my other ideal life. Well anyways,
here we go.

Now You Know How it Feels

"I'll love you forever."

He was lying at the foot of my bed
when he expressed the words I had always
wanted to hear.
But I did not answer.
I knew it was true.
Both hands pressed to his head.
Tears steaming like the steady drip of a faucet.
Shaking his head slowly from side to side
as to rid an unwanted thought.

"I'll love you forever," he said
in agony.
Tormented by his new truth.
One I knew too well.

un.packing

Maybe if I unpack all of this here
I'll get better.
Maybe then life will go on.

Chelsea Pier

You knew I loved the ocean
so you took me to the sea.

Wild, unpredictable, but ultimately free.

The waves and I were touching, the mist had
frizzed my hair.

Dancing and exclaiming, shouting to the air:

"Nature will try to separate us!
But you wouldn't even dare!"

the Human Experience

Who am I to judge you for your
human experiences?

For your fatal flaws and built up walls
For trauma
and relapse
and toxic indulgences.

The soul is so much more than what the body
does to survive
the human experience.

Honey - Jack

Before I knew you the way I do now, I leaned
over and whispered in your ear.
It was the sweetest song to leave my lips.
It could have dripped as honey.
If you kissed me, it would be sweet to the taste.
The warm burn of whiskey filled me up.
I can see us sitting there in a crowded basement.
In white plastic chairs.
Florescent lights hanging from the poles.
You could smell the lack of judgment
leave my lips.
The liquid courage I did not need.
I was sure enough in what I was about to say.
My words were like a gnat buzzing in your ear.
Me, an entire fly.
You liked hanging out.
But there was no way in hell this was something
you wanted to hear.
Or know.
Or make real for you.
By any means.

Self - Sabotage

There's something to be said about being so
incredibly lost, but knowing all the answers
are inside of you. About having the love you have
always wanted, yet keeping walls up to protect
yourself from uncertainty. When you'd rather
choose sabotage and interfere with the flow of life
than to let the joy of the Universe's mysteries
unfold.

Because at least you're the reason for your loss.
Because at least you're the one who opened the
door for misery and let him in.
When you need control that badly.
To be so afraid to fall that you'd rather hang on to
fear because the grasp is more secure.

Sure

I knew then.
I have always known.
And you always knew that I did.
And you always knew you could not handle
something so
inexplicably
undeniably
sure.

Freedom Rings

All of my being wanted to be free more than
anything.
Free in the truest sense.
Not just for a while or until someone flooded my
mind again.
But, I wanted to shed demons like skin.
I knew that meant I'd have to visit places
more unknown than
whatever lived under the bed.
That held memories so repressed I had to decipher
between dreams and reality.

But for freedom, I would go there.
I am freeing myself from the desolate and dismal
compulsion that surrounds my mind and
consumes me.

That sucks me in like a vacuum.
Swallows me whole.

Goodbyes

I never thought goodbye would be easy until it
was the only option that made sense. Until easy
did not matter and I mattered more.

I started to find hope for love outside of you.

Honey, I Shrunk Myself

Honey, I had to shrink to be in your narrative.
Make myself real small.
I only began to notice when I wrote my own.
One where I fit.
Perfectly.

taurus Moons

Until I witnessed our need for this love to stay
alive, I had never known anything to be more
stubborn than you and I.

aijah monet

Seawall Chronicles Part I

I saw you again.
We inspected one another in the dim luster
provided only by the moon and dome lights in
your jeep. Looking for inconsistencies and
searching for the person we had known to love
our whole life. Our eyes moving quickly over one
another, switching back and forth, trying to
ensure that somehow we were still in there.
Trying to assess whether or not you still saw me
the way I saw you.

When you spoke your voice trembled.
I listened closely.
You were talking for a while,
But, in between the tears you were holding back
and the discomfort in your speech, I had a
thought of my own.

I envisioned myself standing there.
And when they asked what happened *this time*,
I'd reply happily,

"I love him."

And oh, how I loved him...
And that would be enough.

D.A.R.E

They said don't you dare
Try a cigarette
Not even once
You'll be addicted after just one puff
Yet I put you between my lips,
lit you on fire,
and inhaled you
Filling my lungs with your fumes
You were cool like Camel
Your menthol coated wounds.

They said don't you dare
Not even casually
You'll be addicted
You'll be dependent
No matter where you are
who you're with
or what you're doing
You can't deny the craving.

Yet, still, I took *the*
longest
most deadly
drag of
you.

Intermission: A Note to My Book

I haven't forgotten about you
I just thought I found my way
Now here I am again, not certain that he'll stay.

So I must go on, un.packing
I guess I stopped too short
Just a few more things to sort through
To understand some more.

Resurrection

The discourse in my head had the power to
welt...with every personal blow I took to myself.
The pressure I put on my being, submersed me
below the surface. So low, the bottom of the sea
could recount. *So I slid sluggishly to the floor of the tub
to grasp if this was true.* My wet rubbery skin
descending against the back of the chilling tile.
Squeaking in resistance. The only resistance there
was. *To hear the tales the bottom of the sea told.*
I closed my eyes. I didn't hear a thing,
but I saw it all.

My lifeless body was being violently tossed around
the ocean floor. I had no control nor did I seek to.
Who knew how much peace came from *letting go.*
Fully conscious, but there was no fight from me. I
shut my eyes. Let the saline water enter every void
space. Burning and filling them completely.

*Dear God, do what you will with me. I let go. Thank
You, Dear God, you can take me now. I'm okay now.*

I opened my eyes. Stinging with irritation, cracking and splitting like shucking an oyster. Tired eyes after being crusted shut and pried open. Welcomed back by the orange and blue static and orbs that come with the unfamiliarity of sight. I had washed back up to shore. *No.* I pounded my weak fists on the sand, barely causing the tiny soil to jump and called out in agony, "No! Dear ocean, I was yours! *I was yours...* I came to hear the tales. I was supposed to be a part of the epic..."

So pitiful and hopeless, even the water doesn't want me.

And I felt a welt emerge.

Or maybe it did and could not keep me. I too, am just too deep and just too dark. And just maybe we were two of the same. And just maybe I'm the one the land needs.

Sometimes I feel like the only way to get better is to be quiet.

I'll tell you What it is

I begged you to tell me you stopped loving me.
That you didn't anymore.
That you fell out of love.
I shoveled the words into your mouth like sand.
You held them there for some time.

Then opened your mouth and spit them back out.
Scraping them from your tongue.

You fucked up and it was a million other things
but that was not something that was true.

As much as I wanted it to be,
You loved me just the same.

Of course you fucking did.

Feel

An arrangement so beautiful
it'd brand me an artist...

I was in search of the perfect sequence of words
when I realized that really, I may never pick them
the way they should be selected.
And that they may not jump off the page
and into your heart.
But that sometimes the beauty is what's felt,
not what's said.

It's in between the lines.
It's after you turn the page
and close the book
because you can't take the rigid truth
in my messy words.

Sitting there, with all of the things
you had once buried.

2018

I felt like people stopped understanding me
and then I soon realized
I had stopped understanding myself.
I lost control and regained it the very next day.
I fought hard for what I believed in and then
learned quickly
where my effort was not welcome.
I learned self-sabotage and I were closer than any
friendship I'd ever kept.
I didn't realize how unnatural self-love was to me
until I was instructed to worry about myself.
And who was that?
I stood up for myself and crumbled under gazes.
I'd build others up and tear myself down in the
very next breath.
I saved lives by 8:00 a.m.
Talked strangers off the ledge by noon
and plotted my own demise by 11:00 p.m.
In a routine fashion with repetitive thoughts,
a way out, and no
way to self soothe.
The person in control you couldn't see,
but it was not me.
That was 2018.

Stargirl

I wanted to be a star but I didn't trust my light.
I gleamed and I shined but only late at night
When no one could see me and nobody knew
That everything I wanted, I saw that in you.

So I hid in your shadow and we shared something
bright. When really it was yours, and I lacked all
the might, to get what was mine, and do it myself,
so I stood there with you and combined all our
wealth.

The easy way out, I then had no fixing.
From afar, how we glistened, but up close I was
missing. I wanted to be more, it was sitting on my
tongue. Like gasping for air with perfect, healthy,
lungs. I wanted to be more than a star in your sky.
Confidence was vibrant, there were no more lies.

It was that, or I go out the star way.
I explode and I die.

these two

It wasn't pretty all the time
Maybe not even half of the time
But the only thing no one could deny was that
It was absolutely magnificent how the two would
choose each other
over and over
again and again.
Always leaving room for one more chance.

Insane or perfectly balanced?
Pitifully attached or ruthless and resilient in love?
Well, that was up to the viewer to decide.

But it was absolutely magnificent how the two
would choose
each other
over and over
again and again
Always leaving room for fate.

I Want to Believe You

c O c O o N
The layer I created to shield me from the pain
I began to peel my shell back
I didn't let anything in
Not a feeling
Not a hum of the truth
Words would ricochet off of me like a force field
You could no longer penetrate me
I am stronger than that
You could no longer tear me down
My wall is higher than that
I had handled the problem except
Leaving no room for me to escape

Nomad

Yearning for a fresh start
For new beginnings
Where it looks or feels nothing like this
Where no one knows me
But me
And finally I am myself
And I am free
And I am new
And I have space
And I have clarity
I can breathe again

Moving On

Whoever you might be
I hope you're out there
It's getting harder out here alone

Knapsack

And so I began to slow my steps
and one by one remove
the straps digging into my shoulders
Feeling the weight drop, shifting from one arm to
another, forcing my body lower
At some point, this load got too heavy to carry
That point? I couldn't tell you when.

That's the thing about all of this
Time and space fuse together
You've gotten so far and you don't know how.
With all of this pain? With all of this baggage?
Did it hurt this bad all along?
Or just when you stop to assess the damages?

You loved me when no one else did and I
can't put into words what that did for me.

aijah monet

Suicide

I'd imagine
The world would go cold
When my flame went out

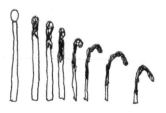

Sorry

Everything I did
I did just to avoid this feeling
The feeling I have now
Hollow chest
Blurred vision
Staring upwards
Wondering if I did something wrong.
Knowing that I did.
Wondering if I'll always feel this alone.
Knowing that I won't.
Maybe that's my karma
Maybe I should.

the Writing Process

This process has forced me to be a willing visitor
to a place I tried desperately to escape from.
I showed back up to a foreign yet familiar place of
pain. Pen and paper in hand.
I read the words on the walls like a tourist.
The stories I had locked away and let enfold my
heart and disturb my mind.
I had to feel it again in order to say what I needed
to say. I had to look myself in the face and
acknowledge that what I felt was real and that this
did happen. Numb and hollowed by this pain.
The journey felt exhausting.

to My Accidental Lover

When you talk to me do you say what you can
or do you say what you mean?
We can't afford any more mistakes.
So please…you stay where
you are and I'll stay put too.
I'll think of your hand lightly grazing my back as
you led me into a night I can now only recall.
I'll think of you from across the bar where I saw
you for a moment and everything inside me
melted. I'll think of all of the mysteries only us
two would uncover given
the chance we'd never take.
Fighting to release a tension we can't put into
motion. You know what I'd rather do
but would never dare.
It's better it was only my back and not my thigh.
It's better you left me wondering why.
So say what you can so we never
do what we want.

Mom

When I was 3 feet tall
someone asked me how I was born and I told
them she made me all on her own.
I was so proud of that.
Argue if they will...
Yet no one challenged me.

I love you

I can't be with you,
No
Not now
But what I really mean is
No
Not ever
You see,
It dawned on me
That if I did that
It would kill me.

Escape Plan

Here's how this is going to go:

I'm going to love you for the rest of my life.
But I'm going to leave you.
And I'm going to leave you now.

I hope your heart lives somewhere it's welcome.

You deserve a love that you don't have to convince even you to see.

un.packing

I didn't want to think the thought of love
I'd crumble
I'm so good without it
I'm
so
good
without
it

Missing you was like crying for a reason I
don't know on a night I couldn't remember.
That doesn't tell you much.
But it tells you everything.

In the Pursuit of Self - Soothing

Sitting here at 2 a.m.
Where I'd usually run to you
Sending a text
You would not answer
Not until the morning
Because you were not on standby
The way I'd hope you'd be

Sitting here at 3 a.m.
Waiting until the knots in my stomach
come undone
Like a schoolgirl's shoelaces,
chasing after the boy,
who wanted to play with dirt
Waiting until the war between my mind, heart,
and the night sky
called a truce
shook hands and released me as prisoner

Sitting here at 4 a.m.
I knew you wouldn't be here much longer
Not because you couldn't
but because I wouldn't have you stay

It gets tiring running after someone who will never be still.

the Reassurance I Needed

You'd say I was your first love and you'd always
feel this way.

You'd never say I was your only love, that'd you'd
be here to stay.

Even the Moon Gets Jealous

To you, I am the moon
Out of reach but close enough to see
You stretch your eye out like a telescope
Trying to observe every dip and hollow that
covers my surface
Making sure there are no new holes
To you, I will always be there even when I don't
want to be seen
You don't have that right
To even look at me
You gave that up when you fell for the sun
When you chose the warmth of her rays
Over the comfort of my craters

Distance Makes the Heart Grow tired

I used to think it was beautiful that if love was
meant to be it would find its way.
Like love had a road map and it knew that
if and always when
it got lost
it could turn around and resume the course.
The romantics of two souls
that would always be one.
No matter who else the other slept with and
swapped intimate energies.
You turned our love into a cliché and hummed it
to me like a lullaby.
Soothing my colicky nights with the most
beautiful platitudeude in the love language.
It drew trite and it stopped calming my storms.
And darling I am a writer.
And we are taught never to use
clichés in our writing.
They're overused.
They're generalizable.
They're impersonal.
The exact number our love now sang.

Pyrite

I would always see him that way.
Out of eyes that sparkled like lightning-struck
opal. Like he had dug out every crater in the
moon's face and sat upon the sun and aligned
each ray that stretched down to caress Earth.

The pain felt like the bottom of a careless sole
splitting through a neatly placed nail
when expecting the warmth of summer grass.

The nights spent rending holes into cotton sheets.
Wrenching away from the emptiness that filled
my sunken chest. Using depressive strength to
muzzle the rage deep within the tight but wobbly
fists of linen that I hung onto. There was boiling
pressure in my face from stifling sobs, screams,
and the unsolicited visuals of you touching them.
Only ivory skull fighting the resistance that kept
my skin from busting right down the middle.
Sometimes I'd check the mirror to see if perhaps
it had.

un.packing

I would always meet his gaze or the sound of his
voice with the heart-pounding excitement and
the stomach-churning uneasiness of discovering
something remarkable and completely
unexpected. Like the first butterfly had sprung
from its cocoon and took flight
to realize it wasn't over for her after all.

I would always see him that way.
Out of bleary eyes. The way the tattered woman
in her precarious garden where
potatoes won't grow sees
Fool's gold.

It stopped being love so long ago.

un.packing

I wanted to know everything about you.

So I could love you a little more than
I should have

So I could love you a little more than you wanted
me to. Since I had no business loving you at all

A Refuge Paradox

I crawled back to broken places.
Looking for shelter to protect me from a storm
I had weathered up myself.
And you were there.
You were always there.
Holding the umbrella I didn't deserve.

Synchronized Souls

A universe apart
You'd trip and I'd fall

Choices Part I

Every day I've been making the choice of
love over resentment
truth over lies
courage over fear
me over this.

Chapter two

In the middle I lost it all

If I ran to a place farthest from *us*
I'd only get closer to *you*.

Sexting

I got my thrill from the promises
made in the heat of lust.
Nothing had gotten me into more trouble than
my way with words after dark.
I was just a writer. Realistic fiction.
No intentions of seeing the midnight
in my stories come to life.

aijah monet

tongue - tied

No matter who you are
you'll taste me on his lips.
Don't stop
keep kissing
Drown me out the way he has to
Focus
Taste the nectar
it's mine
Get lost in one another
But I'm right there
If he pulls slightly on your bottom lip
Know I taught him that
If suddenly he becomes aggressive
It's because he's fighting against the memory
of me
Do something
Now.
To remind him it's you there
Or he might forget.

Caught up in the battle of me.
You kiss him and he'll force himself not to think
of us.
But I'm sure you've learned by now,
The way his mind wanders.
You'll ask him in confidence to never speak of
me.
That's something you two will have to agree
upon.
But it won't last.
For either of you.
He goes to answer your request and you'll find
I'm all over his tongue
I'm present in his phonetics.
He can't make a decision without consulting with
me first.
Whether I'm there or not
I'm in his head
But I did not ask to be.
I'm sorry dear.
But, you cannot know him without meeting me.

to You, Avec Amour, from France
Part II

I write most of this lying in bed or watching out
the window. I'm in France and it's raining hard
here. It's my favorite weather when I'm
comfortably inside. This reminds me of the
weather that I would love to love you in. Before
my dreams get carried away, this is the weather
I would like to wake up to, with you, in the
morning. In our one-bedroom apartment. Small
kitchen, small bathroom, but lots of love. We'd
have a big enough bed for the both of us. It'd be
early in the morning, perhaps the thunder has
woken us up. Let's say 4 a.m. It's still dark and all
we can hear is the loud droplets against our
window. You pull me closer and caress my face.
Something along the lines of what you've always
done to insinuate that you want to kiss me. I'm
still convinced you got it from Twitter but you
claim otherwise. I keep my eyes closed. You come
in closer. I am awake. My eyes are still closed.
You use your finger as a calming pencil and trace
around my face. Randomly and then to mimic the
lines of my mouth. Pulling it into a smile as if my
cheeks and lips were attached to a string and you
were pulling it. At the corner of my lip and
pulling upwards. I don't know what about it

makes me smile…the tickle of your finger against my mouth or my love for the idea that maybe you just want to see me smile. So I smile, naturally. It's hard not to. You pull me closer and we are face to face. I feel your breath against my mouth and your lips slightly brush against my bottom lip. I begin to feel it in the depths of my womb. Tighter. Almost resisting the idea of you. Yet, followed by a new sea. A sailboat designed to be filled. Contradicting, yet most things are. I wonder if you can tell. I'm throbbing, but do you know that? Thunder strikes again. Consistent with my heartbeat when you're this close to me. I open my eyes and ours lock. Have you even taken yours off of me? I think you know what's next. You lick your lips and I smile softly. Ever so softly and back to my natural state. You know this is my favorite time of day to make love. When I'm conscious enough to know I want you but drowsy enough to let you control every part of me. At this time in the morning, it's just you and me. It's our lusty secret. The secret that we can't even stay asleep long enough before we want each other again. It's our lusty secret when we wake up again after all of that pleasure and know we were closer than ever just a few hours prior. In the dark of the morning, our bodies meet and I get to feel you again. Under the drops of rain and silent moans. This is my perfect morning.

Introduction to Women Writers

She was a flower
Like the one tattooed on her left calf.
On the spring day in class
I noticed because the weather broke and she wore
a jean skirt.
We were studying women's literature
So maybe I was heightened.
Aroused by the floating aura of
enchanting women.
"I Am an Emotional Creature" and you are too.
Side by side we recite, "Still I Rise"
and dissect, "The Yellow Wallpaper."
I wanted to talk to you but I couldn't.
You were far more than I could grasp.
Petals bursting from my fingertips as I scribbled
down your name.
I got it from the attendance sheet you passed me.
I longed for you the way the women we read
longed to be heard.
I wanted you but did not know what I'd do with
you if in fact, you wanted me too.
You were doing the thing only boys did to me.
Made me nervous.
Made me silly.
Made me mute.
Made me write.

A Promise I Can Keep

I want to live in a home where we make the rules together. We can laugh, cry, and scream freely. No matter what is said or done, love is the guiding force. Forgiveness is essential and loyalty the only policy. As easy as that sounds, that will not always be the case. Things will not always be good. We will not always agree with one another. We may even fight more than we love for some periods of time, but please know I love you.

Even the snow cried when the sun pressured
it to be something it wasn't ready to.

Catalina State Park

Her soul began to expand in the desert heat of
Arizona. She saw life exist with little rain for
cleansing. Something she believed could be the
only way the broken mended and the shriveled
grew. She thought rain was the only way planted
seeds, bloomed flowers, and how life on Earth
served plentiful. Until she saw cactus draw blood
and also sprout petals of yellow, out of spiky green
arms. The dust bounced and danced. Lightly
coating everything in sight. *Breezy. Swaying in
the air…* welcoming the broken. Those deprived
of water. Those who needed another way.

Connecticut

I never healed at home
Only in the sky
Above the pain
Confused and bewildered by
The kindness of strangers
And the possibilities of a new start
There was so much more out there
I didn't know that until I left the state I was in

un.packing

My world opened up when I realized there was
love outside of you.
Not in people.
But in places.

this Skin I'm in

It was when I realized my weight did not define me, but I could define my weight, that I had no choice but to love every lb. of me.

Central

No one wonders what the shy girl thinks
without thinking about what it feels like to be
inside her too.

Regrets

I bet you regret loving me now. If you knew
I couldn't let go would you have agreed to grasp
my palm and interlock our fingers? Taking the
time to figure out which way felt right. Switching
if necessary. Would you have allowed me to climb
you like a sturdy oak tree, rest in the hollow of
your collar bone the way a newborn chick fills a
nest? Would you let me write you the long love
notes I did? Would you respond and slip them
between the windshield wiper blades on my
ancient Chevy in our high school's parking lot?
Making you Prince Charming in the romantic
narrative that was destined to be satire. Would
you? If you knew they'd end up serving as the
outline for this manuscript? If you knew I'd recite
your praises in my head like scripture. Guiding
me through the world. A world without you in
my life. I bet you regret loving me. Now that this
can't be undone. Now that I've hung on to every
word you've muttered and turned it into art.
I hope you see it was never meant to go against
you. I bet you regret loving me now. Now that
you see what it meant. Meant not only for me.
But for both of us. Now that you loved me too.

*"I didn't ask you to love me.
I didn't ask for any of this."*

What I Learned From those who let me Kiss them

We had just begun to become rooted in one
another. Exploring wet and dry land. Tasting the
sweet hint of exchange. You were afraid of my
soft pink petals before they had even bloomed.
The way they sat perfectly below my nose. Full
and swollen. From tugging and sucking.
They burned of rose and honey. Even in the
moment we released. Just to regain oxygen.
I longed to be entangled. I leaned in for more.
Water me. Nurture me. And I will help you grow.

You dodged my kiss and my soft pink petals
crumbled and dissipated into the darkness like
ashes.

I had fallen forward, clumsily, shocked, by your
sudden move. Expecting your lips. Opening my
eyes now. Embarrassed and confused.

I looked to you like a child searching for answers.
You lifted my chin and kissed me gently.
It was you who could plant your lips on mine.
And we could become entwined in that.

But I could not kiss you. For that would mean something entirely different.

A few years later. I was showing you how to kiss.

I'd stop you as you leaned in. Or dodge you as you'd lean forward, eyes closed, expecting my lips. But only catching the air. You'd look up furious.

Denial lacks sugar cane my sweetness.

Not like *that*.

Like this.

aijah monet

And even still
Only those who have loved
At an acute severity…
To feel
pain
in
love
can understand
how even still
My love goes on
How even still
On that cold night in March
My heart cried out for you

93

Please don't ever settle for being half-wanted.
From my broken heart to yours.

He hadn't stopped breaking my heart. Why you ask? Well, dear, because I hadn't stopped letting him.

Attachment theory Part I

The adult in me does not want you.
The child in me weeps.

What I Wish I Didn't Know...

And at the end
our love taught me everything.
Everything
I needed to know
about everything
love was not.

So that I Could Still Choose You

"My goodness!"

I assured him that this was not what love felt like.
That when he knew, he wouldn't doubt it.
That he'd know he had met her when he couldn't
imagine doing anything he'd done to me to her.
And I only knew that, because I loved him in that
same way.

I didn't want it to hurt.
But it had to.

In Spite of You

I should hate you and you know that.
My revenge is leaving enough time and space
between us.
I want you to ponder over my absence
Until you trace your finger along the brim of
insanity and hear it sing.
You'll try to convince yourself that I was honest
in my expression of eternal love.
But I should hate you and you know that.
So you'll question it.
And you'll regret what you've done to cut me to
the marrow.
You could see my bone.
You read each page like you're looking for
something you dropped.
You won't find the answer.
And I don't want you to.
That silence you produced where I needed words
the most...
When I asked you why...
You tortured me in the name of love.
I return, that same stillness to you,
When you wonder if I could possibly hate you,
Knowing that I should.

Wildfire

You tapped into the most vulnerable me.
She's 16 and she loves you like the peak of a
wildfire.

Bon Appetite

You said to understand what you did to me you should read every word of my deepest thoughts. Maybe then, you could understand the pain you knew you too needed to feel. So we could finally be equal. Then, you could understand what you had done to me. As if you had not been there when you did it.

Anyways.
Here you are.

You Paved the Road to Hell

The road to Hell was paved with good intentions.
That is what you told me.

But before you picked me up, you painted the sky
with clouds of blue and night's canvas with the
Big Dipper. You splattered the Milky Way with
stardust and planted Monet's Water Lilies in the
passing lakes. We made love at the rest stops.
You traced my mouth with fingers of a puppeteer.
Your prickly touch swiftly causing the corner of
my lips to curl into a smile. You turned up the
dial and played our song down the endless
winding road you used your hands to pave. Rain
or shine. Hand on thigh. Heart in pocket.

the tears of a Knowing Heart

Today I regret the advice I give but don't take.
As my eyes are swollen shut from the well of tears
pulled up by the strength of my shaky arms
from the depths of my sunken heart.
Sadness is wrapped around me.

Into tomorrow Mourning Part I

The pain is waking up and feeling peace.
Knowing you cried yourself into blue jays
chirping and the sun pulling back your curtains
and peeking through the glass.

The heartache in knowing you felt better asleep.

Now I lay me Down to Sleep

I prayed that God would spare me from the pain.
I had concluded that I was not strong enough to
bear it. And I accepted that. I asked him to kill me
in between the time I took my last fully conscious
breath. Kill me after falling asleep in a sea of tears
but before the sun passed through my eyelids and
burned my cornea. Peacefully.

Take me then. Gently and swiftly. In the way that
no one would notice. In the way, they already
don't. I thanked Him for the life I had lived but
was no longer interested in seeing this one
through. It'd be better if I went with You. I fell
asleep to this melodic discourse with God. And I
woke up to the suns heat burning my lids.

I cried and I cried and I cried *and I cried…*

I was awake. The pain of another day.
I learned strength when I had none.
When I suffered in silence and had no choice but
to survive…

Because God wouldn't take me.

Chapter three

And in the end I finally realized

Grounding

If I write about right now
I smell bacon cooking
The rumble of my heater
Zoë snores her way into morning
Everything's blurry
I don't have my glasses on yet
I'm typing these words
The garbage truck has come

If I wrote about right now
I don't think of you.

Inching

I kept the remnants of my cocoon dangling
from my wing
In case the fear of flying crept back in
Like a parachute in case I fell
I could somehow reverse back into the tight
confines of comfort.

The wind laughed
And the birds nipped at my blanket
But for dear life, I held on to the fragments of my
old home.

Not realizing the sky was my sanctuary
Or how silly I looked holding onto what was.

The bees spread the message
The wind carried it home
The birds were showing me the way
And finally, I let go.

un.packing

You're fading my dear
From my mind again
I can't hear you in my head
And the things that you told me,
I can no longer recite
It was your words I hung onto
There was nothing else to grasp
I can't make out your voice
I can't recall your tune
The memories
The time
The jokes
The notes
The car rides
The dates
The sky the day we met
The moon the night we first made love
The sweet nothings
The regrets
The confusion
The false hope
The lies
Her
You're fading dear
You're gone
You lost me.

Select all Delete

Hey,

We were both.

Holy like Heaven. Cool like the other side of the
pillow and the nook in the bed where your body
heat hadn't spread to yet.

Humid like Hell. Struggling to breathe.
Fumes filled your throat. Cotton mouth but
taking the last normal breath to choke out

"You're mine."

Do you think we'd be Co-Dependent
in Every Life?

Legacy Part I

The last word in this book signifies our end. I will leave our love enclosed in these pages and will not drag it out another syllable. It will always exist but this cannot go on. I gave it a home that's safe. That's forever. That's what we wanted yet what we could not provide. So here it is. In these thin wooden sheets dipped in ink clouds of thought. I'm sorry that this is it for us. That our story cannot go on. That the last word in this book is how we will end the tale. So close the book. Hold it tight. Let it out. Wail. Because it hurts like hell. It hurts me to write this. To know that you'll read this. And frantically search for more pages. More words. More meaning. More us. We've failed the test of time. So I'll leave us here.

Why Love Should Belong to Adults

People never squatted down in the tall grass
facing green blades, stared at my petals, and
thought, "*This one. This is the one I will choose.*"
I was never the flower the boys picked.
So I grew and I grew from never being chosen.
Envying the Daisy squashed in the sweaty palms
of youth. Knowing she'd make a human girl
squeal in excitement. Seeing that I only buzzed
with the bees and rolled with the polies. Not
knowing that they were picked for their petals
and cross-pollination. Only left to die that same
day by ungrateful creatures. And that there was
so much good in being left to grow.
I am tall. I kiss the sky.
I will never be uprooted to fill the palm of one
who thinks they can take me from where I have
started without sitting beside my stalk,
talking to me daily, watering my leaves,
visiting my spot in the grass, and asking me
if I would do the honors of letting them
choose me. Take me home in a vase of water
and don't ever forget to tell my petals how
beautiful they are in the spring and be prepared
to catch them as they fall in January.

Anything v. Nothing

You gave me your worst.
I begged for more.

Bloodline

I'm sitting with a lump of pain in my chest.
Afraid that it will never go away.
Because even on the best days, the pain of the
memories we did not get to make,
settles into my veins.

More than Life Itself

I will love him for the rest of my life and
I don't know where to place that feeling.
It doesn't fit in my mind
It is the depth of the ocean.
It doesn't fit in my heart
It is the entire universe
It couldn't fit in this lifetime
It just isn't long enough

Annecy - le - Vieux

I left our love locked somewhere safe.
Somewhere safe and sound.
Where love is sweet like nectar
it hums the sweetest tune

and we cannot be bound
our love can only bloom.

Learning Curve

I'm in a new body
One I don't know well
With extra skin and divots
With rolls and stripes
But I will learn to love it

Strange Fellow

A strange fellow
Misunderstood but absolutely clear
Predictable and calculated but the
mystery's still there
You strum through life
Playing my heart the same way you
move those strings
And I let you do it
And I want it done
It's what we do
You're a strange fellow
and I am too

Mystic

I liked you because you were dark
and I was dark too
but you cared
and that was the thing about you,
the thing I'd follow through life aimlessly.

Hurt People, Hurt People

I became the girls who tortured me.
And only because I could.
And that's when I welcomed the worst version of
myself into existence,
And showed her to the door.

A Casual Sex Poem

Some people will strip you
Strip you bare
Until you are naked
Until you have nothing left
But shared air
And minimal decency

Into tomorrow Mourning Part II

I try and start every morning with a grateful
heart. After a night of compulsively praying to
avoid the darkness and chase the pain away.
I wake up relieved that somehow,
I made it through the worst.

Pillow Princess

Did she feel like velvet?

Was your mouth watering as you looked down to your knees and saw her putting on a show? You looked down at me too, but rarely up at me for my rodeo performance. I bet her, being her, and not me, teased your spirit as you teased her throughout the night. Was she a screamer or did the pillows suffocate her moans? Did you finally get to act out the dreams you saw on screens? I'm sure she moved for you in ways I wouldn't and really didn't want to.

10/10 Do not Recommend

I was going to find her
and when I did
I never knew I would
find me too.

Ghostwriter

DOES SHE KNOW? THAT EVERYTHING YOU TOLD HER, I TAUGHT YOU. THAT I AM THE WRITER AND THAT YOU ARE THE SCRIBE.

o o o

No one Snores Like a Lying man

I'd invite you to bed when your place was the
floor. I tossed and turned all night while you slept
peacefully the way a lying man does.

Holding every truth I needed to know in there
with your dreams.

I'd lie awake not understanding why my peace
was so disturbed. How you used to be my security
blanket and now your presence kept me up.
I'd beg you to help me figure out why I couldn't
sleep and you'd tell me you didn't know.
You knew. Because you were bringing their
energy into my sheets. You were a stranger who
took the form of someone I knew so well.
I couldn't sleep with you because I didn't know
you anymore. You were a living nightmare in
my bed. The sleep paralysis above my head.

A clone of my lover.

I should have known—
your touch was cold.

What happened to you?

What happened? I asked over and over, saddened
by the need for the rhetorical question at all.

You paused.

My palms went cold.
My breath cut short.
My heart began to shatter.
My heat began to rise.

Something had happened.

Your truth set you free
but imprisoned me.

Why
Didn't
You
Just
Tell
Me

I pleaded.

I forgave you already.

Perennial

He started to heal from the years of secrecy
from the regret and discomfort of a double life
He began to bloom again
I could see the evergreen roots overlapping and
replacing black decaying vines
I picked off the dead parts
the water from our tears replenished
buds of personality and affection were reemerging
you could look me in the eye again
I sprinkled forgiveness over the soil
He began to bloom again.

Pop - Quiz

I don't know what hurt more.

    A. You are choosing her

    or

    B. Me choosing you

Answer: *A. You choosing her*

She was just like me.
Which made me hate you
Which made me hate her
Which made me hate me

Detroit

I lost my mind. I admit that.
You drove me there and dropped me off.
Can you admit that?

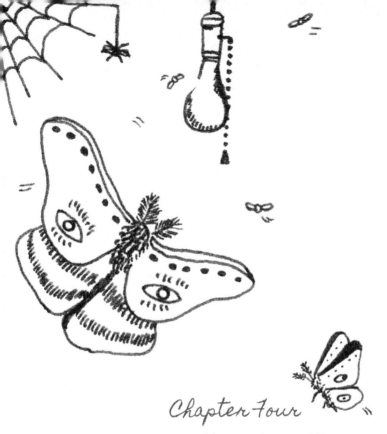

Chapter Four

You would never let me fall.

aijah monet

When You're in Love

It sent me spinning
Remembering what it feels like when
It's true for both of you.

Seawall Chronicles

Part II: Lordship

There were days filled with sunshine and infinite
kisses. Just you, me, and the sea. You couldn't
keep your mouth from meeting mine. The ocean
and the coast guffawed in awe. Even they could
not keep up. They stopped trying and rolled in
slowly. The seafoam crackled in admiration.
Your lips crashing against mine knocking me off
balance but you'd catch me by the base of my hips
and bring me in for the embrace of another wave.
Grazing your bottom lip over mine and closing it
over. Kissing in between smiles, lightly bumping
teeth, and struggling against the strain of your
cheeks. Because bliss and desire were the best of
friends. Your eyes closed and sometimes opened.
I'd catch your gaze. That look. Wide-eyed.
Like the world had suddenly stopped for you.
I couldn't tell if you were afraid or amazed.
It was both. Like after years of being in your
company you finally saw me.

This is the girl I have been with…
And God, do I love her.

That look met mine and my entire body braced.
I'd stop grinning and stare right back.
As if the world had suddenly stopped for me too.

This boy loves me more than his own good...
And oh how dearly I love him back.

I don't know what got into you on those days,
but I wouldn't stop it for a second. We'd roll
around in the dandelion fields a few feet from the
beach. You'd lay on your back as daylight broke.
A hundred summer gnats were gossiping about
our love in the patch of grass beside us.
You kissed me once for each of them. They
swooned and buzzed in excitement at the show.
And when your lips got tired, the corner of your
mouth returned to a sweet smile...you'd press
your lips out, eyes tightly shut...I think you used
to pretend I wasn't there to be greeted with the
excitement of once more, meeting you with me.
The sweet smile of a boy who loved a girl.

When we Define it

I loved you in the literal sense of the word
In all of the ambiguous and confusing parts too

to You, Avec Amour, from France
Part III

Thank you for being my best friend. For allowing me to always be myself. To say what I feel. To cry uncontrollably almost every time we talk. To love me even when I'm covered in tears. To tell me I'm beautiful when I'm crying the most. To leave class and sit on the phone with me when I'm lower than I've ever been. To hold my hand as tight as you can when I wanted to let go, to stop fighting, to stop living. Thank you for allowing me to feel everything that I have in this lifetime. There is no me without you. I know I will survive with or without you. I'm not sure how. I can't truly say. But one thing that I am absolutely sure of is the fact that my best shot at a full life is one where you're by my side. You make being alive so nice.

I would like to occupy someone's space.

aijah monet

Legacy Part II

Our love birthed a book
A romance before its time
One where its mother lives through the labor
and tells the tale herself.

Symptom Picture

A snake. I slithered out of the sheets I had been shedding in for 48 hours. You could build another me in what I had left behind. Days filled with self-loathing and despair. Nights of rumination and compulsive thoughts. Hell had nothing on the mind that occupied my skull. Yet, like clockwork, daylight broke and it was Wednesday. I couldn't stand to see myself in the mirror. But I walked over anyway. Staring at a lifeless reflection. Mocking my pity. The carcass of a girl who you'd think only knew dread. Looking me in the eyes. Staring into my face. I smiled for the first time in two weeks. Not out of happiness or anything remotely automatic, but in memory. Just to see what it used to feel like to do such a thing. I was afraid that maybe I had forgotten what it felt like to smile. Forcing my cheeks wider. Stretching my jaw. Unnatural and bizarre. Why couldn't I be normal? My lips had not parted from a straight line in 14 days. Not to speak. Not to cry. Definitely not to smile.

And I began to dance.

I danced. And I danced for my life. Flailing my body parts around. Shaking the pain away.

Kicking the tension. A shift no man nor God
could predict. The anxiety floated off my skin like
dust in the sunlight. The depression lifted from
the depths of my shoulders and lining of my gut.
Fleeing from me like dew emerging from the
grass in the mist of the morning. I danced. And I
laughed a real laugh. And smiled a real grin. And I
danced. And I danced. And I fucking danced.
Gaining control of my limbs. I stood back in front
of the mirror. Looking me in my eyes. Watching
my chest rise and fall under my breast. I was stoic
but for the first time, I was stunned and frankly
alarmed by my own behavior. Organically, like
the first bud pushed out of a root, I thought to
myself:

I am bipolar.

the Weight in Waiting Part I

Breathing. I couldn't breathe without the weight of sadness resting its heavy palms against my diaphragm. Resuscitation. In full irony, killing me with each compression.

I wondered what it would be like if it lifted its hands. But the weight was what I'd always known. I'd die with the force of sadness beaten into my chest.

to You, Avec Amour, from France
Part IV

I think I'll stop now. I want you to know I'll be
okay if this is not my life. I will make a way. Just
know I will never stop dreaming in this way. This
is my fairy tale. The fairy tale I know still exists. I
have learned that dreams come from your heart,
not from anything else. No human error, no
flaws, no pain can truly disturb your dreams.
Maybe momentarily but never forever. If that
does happen you have lost your faith. So even if it
is not you, I will be okay. The narrative may
change and maybe I won't want chickens
anymore or maybe I'll just want a condo. But
know that I will never stop dreaming. When they
ask of the perfect love story no matter who I'm
with I will tell the one of you and me.

un.packing

I will not tell you how to love yourself if I am still learning. But please try anyways and I will too.

My expectations were for us to grow.
And I learned the reality of expectations on a
humid day in May.
Where our leaves broke off
You shriveled up
and I died.

A reality where the first cloud to notice didn't cry
until Autumn.

Into tomorrow Mourning Part III

We learn what we want from what we didn't receive. From puffy eyes and stained cheeks we didn't deserve.

Cancer Sun

There is so much comfort in knowing
that despite all else
my heart is pure.

Love and kindness will always feel like home.

Super 8

I'll blink away your memory when it gets stuck
on replay. I used to play it on repeat to get me
through the day. A final taste of who we were
when things were tried and true. Now the tape. It
won't rewind. I don't know what to do.

the Sweetest Love I Have Ever Known

Waking up
laughing from a dream
Filled with humor you don't remember
You can't explain it
It doesn't make sense
Explaining it anyway
That was loving you

Perfectly cooked eggs
Over medium
Saturday morning
Sloppy Waffle
Spicy Jeff
I like mine scrambled hard
That was loving you

The first snowflake of the season to kiss your nose
My eye and a snowball
It was Chris
He blamed someone else
That was loving you

Sometimes I remember your soul and despite all
else, I know you didn't mean to hurt me like this.
And sometimes I forgive you.
That was loving you.

I would have loved you harder had I'd known
it'd be so easy.

I took a Greyhound for You...
You took one for me too.

We waited for the Greyhound in the middle of a
New England snowstorm. I would get on a bus
and take it anywhere in the world if I thought
you might be there. We stood there hoping it
wouldn't come so we could rush back up to your
bedroom and spend one more night underneath
one another. You were so cold and pale and your
hat was pulled over your ears and goddamn
I loved you. I can still feel the weather on your
lips. I cried all the way home... The bus came
after all. My best friend was behind me and I was
leaving what felt like home. Anywhere you were
felt like home. I should have stopped that bus
driver. I had left something valuable behind.
In a frantic search, I went looking for what I left.
You still had my heart. Soothed by the pulsating
lump in my right pocket. Remembering I had
yours too.

the Power of Secrecy

Nobody knows the pain I felt. And I say that
with blame. No one knew the pain I felt because
I didn't tell anyone. *Why didn't you ask me?*
I didn't tell anyone that my bones rattled with
sadness. *How couldn't you see that under my skin?*
Or that I wasn't eating or that I spent 23 hours of
the day stuck in my mind with the intrusive
thoughts that lead me into this place? *Why didn't
you knock on my door?* Nobody knew the pain I
felt because they couldn't. Because they wouldn't
have. Unless I told them. *Why didn't you save me?*

If I Hadn't Watch them Go,

My mind started to fear people. I thought maybe they could see how sad I was and would want to do something about it. But how could I explain? *This is just who I am now.* So I began to lock eyes with the ground and make my way through the world just like that. Seeing passing feet. Reminding me of everything I had lost. That had simply walked away from me. Just like that.

Did they Really Leave?

the Night the Signs Pointed to Me

The pamphlet read:
"How to recognize someone close to you is
suicidal."
As I read each word the knots in my stomach
doubled.
The lump in my throat got harder and harder to
swallow.
I croaked.
A tear rolled down.
No one noticed.

un.packing

the Weight in Waiting Part II

You
remember,
don't you?
When
the
world
was
so
heavy
sleep
was the
only
thing that
did not
crush your
spine.

160

thank you for showing up for me

To the people who saved me:

Thank you for answering my call.
Thank you for talking me down.
Thank you for telling me what my life meant to
you when it didn't mean a thing to me.
Thank you for sharing our favorite memories.
Thank you for bringing me flowers.
Thank you for laughing when I could only pull a
weak grin.
Thank you for wiping my empty tears.
Thank you for giving me space.
Thank you for forgiving me…
For trying to take my life from you, too.
Way too many times.

un.packing

When I wanted to die I ran to you. As wrong as
you were, you made me feel full. So I think I got
confused. You didn't want me and I don't think
I wanted you. But you had a flashlight in your
heart that always guided me out of the dark.
You weren't mine and I know that. But when
I wanted to die I ran to you like you were.

Joy

I can't tell you the reason or the season I got my joy back. I don't know what the weather was like or the phase of the moon. I can't tell you how many stars were born that night or if the sky was welcoming dusk or dawn. But, the wind told the trees that Heaven shines down on people every once and a while. The cardinal told the blue jay that God sent an angel to return the light that left her soul. He found it in her dreams. Amongst the discourse. On this rare occasion, the holy gates of Heaven creaked open and the angel sent for Earth. She delivered it down, wrapped in cloud, tied in a comet's tail. Traveling through the branches and the leaves, her light, filled every shadow and regrew every fallen leaf. Beyond the tree, the most deserving, the one who lost her spark. And on that day she was returned the power which was always hers. The power she prayed away. It came through the walls, swirled around the grass, fluttered in snow, mixed in her morning tea, on a flower she picked from a field full of weeds, a lemon she squeezed over her dinner.

Wherever I was or whatever I was doing,
my joy had been returned.

un.packing

I don't want to die anymore and I'm sorry that I did.

attachment theory Part II

When you turned to leave I swear all the stars
stopped shining
And crows flew south
The planet stopped spinning and for a second
it was comforting
My worn-out heart slowed its beating.
It was on its last leg anyway.
The buzzing in my ears grew louder.
Was it buzzing or my cells screaming
from within?
The hollow in my stomach dug deeper
The brown in my eyes dulled to grey
I was going to die without you.

If you leave now,
Don't come back again.

Hey, Before you go,

You kissed me goodbye and you told me to never change. To stay beautiful. I nodded my head sadly in agreement and turned to go inside. And babe I tried. I tried not to change when the world around me was pulling at my skin and tugging on my pant leg. Grasping for my zipper, too. Crawling up my neck and climbing into my ear. I promised I wouldn't change, but you did. You changed right before my eyes. I reached out to stop you, but everything moved in slow motion. It sped up for you. I watched you laugh at things that weren't funny and go places when you were tired. You holding girls' hands on the way to house parties. Trying things we swore we never would. I watched you become someone entirely new. Heavy droplets began to swell in the sockets of my eyes, balancing on my lashes. As I watched the footage, I remembered that amid your goodbyes and "see you soons" I didn't ask you not to.

Stay Golden... Stay Beautiful

always

If I loved you once
I will love you always
Beyond a point in time.

Miraculous Recovery!

Did you know a heart can break a million times
and still beat in your chest?
You should see mine go.

Crushes

I loved someone I barely even knew
But my idea of him was stellar

I loved someone I barely even knew
But my idea of her was stellar

un.packing

I'd do it again
Not because I want to hurt anyone
Not because the guilt wasn't overwhelming
But because your place in my life
Eventually taught me how to stop
Stop indulging
Stop giving
Stop antagonizing
Stop flirting
Stop being "friends"
Stop enabling
Stop allowing pain
Stop ignoring triggers
Stop loving people who don't deserve your love
Stop loving people who can't receive your love
Stop loving people who don't want your love
Stop loving people who you don't really love

Very rarely time will pass without the clock
striking you.

the World is Better With you in it

Stay alive. The morning dew still rises above the grass for you. Every lemon grown hopes to make its way to you. Your eyes aren't done seeing from the perspective that is so beautifully yours.

Choices Part II

It wasn't all bad.
He knows that
and
I know that.
There's no one
who can
convince me that
it was not
love.
It was
unconditional
but
we had to make a choice.

No You, No Me

It was his hand that stroked the back of my neck
While I wrote
It was him that pulled the words from the
Bursting heart in my chest
He guided my pen
Our love bled onto these pages.

I Beg of You...

Don't go so soon
I begged
I've got something left to tell you.

I didn't.

Even still
you don't know the pain
or have the answers
that could save me from me.

Please.

You must stay until we sort
through this mess.

I need you.

Don't go
so soon.

You Absolute Masterpiece

Your stomach hangs over your belt
it hasn't done that in a while.
And the skin on your canvas is expanding
and ripping trying to keep you all in.
Your body makes room for you
it tears and it fills and it squeezes you in.

Don't settle for anything that doesn't
bend to keep all of you, you.

Out of Body

Some days it feels like my extremities are
being pulled by
someone else
somewhere else
who wants the worst for me

Cheating

Tell her that it had nothing to do with her.

Be decent and break it to her. You kissed
someone else. And felt someone else. You ran
your fingers through someone else's hair. Pulling
counterclockwise taking a fist of it. Pulling their
head back while they danced for you. Squeezed
their thighs and pulled them into you. Bringing
you closer and closer to convulsion. Because you
couldn't make any other choice in that moment.
That the instincts of your descendants called you.
They howl and you followed.

Be decent and soothe her disgruntled mind.
Remind her that you gambled with her trust for
reasons that go beyond the way she looks in bed.
Grab her back as she walks away. Take her by
both shoulders. Look her in her crying eyes.
You're breaking her. Reassure her that she still
makes you feel good. That she gets on top
enough. That you still vibrate for her. You only
reach peaks with her. When she looks down in
shame. Lift her chin. Tell her that she could shave
or not shave. You'll take her as she comes.
That her body has always driven you crazy.
Don't lose a pound. Your temple feels like home.

She will not believe you. But tell her anyway.
Whatever you do. Leave or stay. Say whatever it
is that she needs to hear. Do not allow this woman
to believe that your inability to control
y o u r s e l f has anything to do with who she is.
This... This is your doing.

Breathe Again

There are going to be days that look like rain
even when the sun is shining.
Anticipating darkness
on the brightest dawns.
When it feels like the atmosphere is closing in on
you and it's getting harder to breathe,
breathe anyway. Space and clarity surround you.
Give yourself a chance to breathe again.

An Inner - Strength Story

Remember that you survived arctic twilights.
Nights spent crying yourself to sleep. Clinging to
the darkness. Bracing for the next shooting pain
from the memories of the past. Clinging to your
knees in hopes that something could keep you
from falling apart. Your tears froze as they fell.
The survivors meeting your top lip. You took
them in. Salt and sadness. The taste was
comforting. It reminded you that you were still
alive. As numb as you felt. Your senses were
intact. It all hurt so badly. Remember those nights.
Where you were pleading with yourself to just
pull it together enough to see the next sunrise.
Where loneliness ate at your gut and rolled
through you like the steam of thawing snow.
Know that you can get through anything.
Because you have. And you did it alone. The only
person who could have dug you out, was you,
climbing from the depths of the desert to reclaim
your frozen host.

Note to Self

It doesn't start to heal until they're gone
Then you miss them when things feel fine
You haven't thought about them in a while
But fight yourself from falling into the same cycle
Don't turn back now
You've been there before

Let me teach you one thing. Be kind to yourself.
There's no guarantee that anyone else will be kind
to you. The world proves that every day. When
hate kills the remarkable and we hurt our home.

Epilogue

June 7th, 2016

Today I woke up feeling incredibly blessed. Not everything is perfect and by no means will it ever be, but I have amazing people surrounding me and great opportunities coming my way. I know that God will never let me fall and that I am so blessed to have gone through that hard time. Many more will come, but right now I'm experiencing the sun. There are so many people for me to thank but, ultimately I came here to advise you to never give up. Not on life, not on love, not on a darn thing. You never know what the next day, month, or year will bring. This journal entry is to thank God for dragging me through and I am happy to be smiling on the other side. Even if it's just for now.

About the Author

Aijah Monet Downer is a writer currently residing in Connecticut. In 2019, Aijah received her Master's in Social Work from Fordham University. She compiled this collection of poems and created an online community in hopes that no one else ever feels alone. She hopes that you too will begin to unpack. With time the load will get too heavy. So she asks, before then, take the time, you too can heal.

To un.pack with Aijah and thousands of others, visit her on Instagram @un.packing or aijahmonet.com.

Contents

aijah monet

a message to myself and un.packing:

Happiness scares you because its fleeting nature feels a lot like
abandonment. Accept the intrusive feeling of sadness in place of the
pride and joy you were once promised. The sadness is in knowing
that the better parts of your life are ahead of you. And there are those
whom you love deeply who will have to stay behind. People who
will no longer make sense if you heal completely. Please heal
anyway. It sets in that warm hellos may also mean chilling goodbyes.
So you hold on a little tighter…for a little while longer. Allow
yourself the hesitation in giving this your all. It's okay to be afraid of
the reality of everything you have ever wanted. It's okay if you
approach the door others run to, slowly and with caution.
Apprehension will not hinder the journey you are on. There is truly
nothing you can do to obstruct your path…to keep you from where
you are headed. It's okay that the good times remind you of
everything you gave up to get here. It's okay that love feels
suffocating. It scares you. You run from it. You opt-out. You fight
it. All in fear that if you choose love, it still may not stay. It has left
before. The fear, however, is not in love, but in loss. You will find
vulnerability alluring again. Be patient, your heart is still healing.
You will love again and in full. That love will come to you.
That love will mend what's broken.

Aijah, people are proud of you. Yet you struggle to understand why.
You thank them and try with all of your being to believe you are
worthy of praise. You save their compliments in screenshots and tuck
them away in your heart and mind in hopes of a day in the future
where it finally feels safe to accept them. A day where the honor will
feel warranted. For now, just know you are reaching people in a real
way. You are doing it Aijah. *You're really doing it…* It's okay that the
truth in this welcomes tears. You don't have to blink them away.
But you will. That's what you do now. Aijah, I hope you remember
what it's like to feel with freedom. Before you allowed them to
shame your sensitivity. Before you too believed it was shameful to be
soft. Meaning it was shameful to be you. I wish it stopped there. We
both know it doesn't. Aijah, cry so you can laugh. Invite anger so
you do not meet rage. Love yourself so you can let them love you
too. Love yourself so you can love whoever you love. I know how

un.packing

badly you want to make it. In love and in success. Never forget that all of this too is an accomplishment. It's okay if success looks different than the picture you have painted in your mind. Starting over is not as scary as it used to be. Here's a blank canvas if you need one. Be kind to yourself. Take your time. This takes time. Destroy the idea that after un.packing there is nothing left to you. There is so much to you, Aijah. I need you to trust your light. It is the same light that led you from the depths of darkness. The same darkness I know just how dearly you miss. Miss it, but you don't get to live there. I hope you learn to love the pretty part. Aijah, I believe this is the pretty part. I hope you learn that you do not have to be in pain to be powerful and that you do not have to be in pain to be a poet. I know people are reading this who are hurting. Hurting merely because you were hurting. People hurting right alongside you and did not realize it until they saw bits and pieces of their story in yours. Wishing they too had a way through... a way to release the weight. Not realizing it was okay to be this honest with themselves until they saw you do it. You have un.packing to thank for that. Lead them from the dark.

And so, un.packing, thank you for holding all the pain in her world. For showing her the magnificence in rock-bottom. Triumph looks so good on her. Thank you for giving her purpose. A purpose she is proud of. Thank you for being the catalyst to everything meant for her. Thank you for making her, her. For showing her how beautiful she is. Stunning, really. How deep her affections run, how her differences and imperfections allow for more love, and how worthy she is of her space in this world. Light is her essence and she would have never known that. Thank you for being there for her, before anyone else. She will turn to you often. Others will too. So long, for now, her beloved friend. Her journey is not complete. She has advanced and regressed. She has withered and bloomed right before your pages. She does not have it all figured out and because of that, she will meet you again, in another way in another time... soon.

I am always getting better. Life has gone on.
I have unpacked it all here. I have found where I belong.
Always & forevermore—un.packing.

Made in the USA
Monee, IL
24 March 2020